THE BOAZ PRAYER

RUTH: ROMANCE, REDEMPTION AND RESTORATION

DR. TAI A. ADEBOYE

the *boaz* prayer

Ruth: Romance, Redemption and Restoration

Dr. Tai A. Adeboboye

CASTLE QUAY BOOKS

The Boaz Prayer—Ruth: Romance, Redemption and Restoration
Copyright ©2012 Dr. Tai A. Adeboboye
All rights reserved
Printed in Canada
International Standard Book Number: 978-1-927355-26-8
ISBN 978-1-927355-27-5 EPUB
Published by:
Castle Quay Books
Pickering, Ontario
Tel: (416) 573-3249
E-mail: info@castlequaybooks.com   www.castlequaybooks.com
Edited by Lori MacKay
Cover design by Burst Impressions
Printed at Essence Publishing, Belleville, Ontario

Cataloguing data available from Library and Archives Canada

Library and Archives Canada Cataloguing in Publication
Adeboboye, Tai A., 1964-
        The Boaz prayer : Ruth : romance, redemption and restoration
/ Tai A. Adeboboye.

ISBN 978-1-927355-26-8
        1. Bible. O.T. Ruth—Prayers. 2. Boaz (Biblical figure).
3. Prayer—Christianity. I. Title.

BS1315.6.P68A34 2012   242'.722   C2012-907213-3

Issued also in electronic format.

ISBN **978-1-927355-27-5**

contents

acknowledgements

To God be the glory for giving me the grace and provision to write this book. Truly it has been a dream come true!

Also, I will be amiss if I fail to acknowledge several amazing people in my life who have been my cheerleaders throughout my "running the race" of putting pen on paper to share what the Lord has been teaching me through the lives of two extraordinary individuals in the Bible—Ruth and Boaz.

Thank you, Marian, my loving wife of 21 years. You have stood by me through thick and thin. What an amazing woman you are!

To my four precious children, Adam, Naomi, Daniel and Isaiah, I thank God for you all daily. You have been a source of inspiration to me in all that I do. Thank you for your patience during the writing of this book.

To my loving congregation, Wilmar Heights Baptist Church, your support and encouragement in affirming the call of God in my life will always be remembered. Thank you for experiencing the truth of the Boaz prayer with me while the message of the book of Ruth was preached to you. I am grateful you spurred me on to write this book. I love you all!

And to all the men and women who are helping to rebuild Wilmar for the glory of God, thank you!

Introduction

Jesus admonishes us to "*Watch and pray*" (Matthew 26:41, NIV). The book you are holding in your hand is about taking your prayer life to a whole new level. I am talking about praying a Boaz-like prayer. You have probably heard of the prayer of Jabez. But have you heard of the Boaz prayer? The Boaz prayer is a little prayer like the prayer of Jabez, found in the book of Ruth.

Before I introduce you to this awesome prayer that has truly revolutionized my prayer life, there are two important warnings we need to "watch" for in the book of Ruth just as the Lord Jesus instructed us to "watch and pray." These two warnings are found in the first chapter of the book of Ruth and are dealt with in the first two chapters of this book.

The rest of the chapters will encourage you to come on an incredible adventure of praying the Boaz prayer daily for yourself, your family and friends. Simply put, the Boaz prayer is a prayer for

God's favour, to be at the right place at the right time, to meet the right person, with the right provision, which will lead to the right partnership, resulting in the providential plan of God for your life. Isn't that an incredible prayer to pray?

Boaz prayed it for Ruth, and as she stood in agreement with the prayer she saw God's transforming power turn her trials into triumph and her mess into a message of romance, redemption and restoration.

I invite you to join me and many others for a personal encounter as we pray the Boaz prayer together. Will you?

CHAPTER ONE

Decisions That Determine Destiny

The book of Ruth is one of those priceless gems you'll find in the strangest of places, hidden in the deep, rugged, dark corners of a place called "nowhere." But like a rose trampled on the ground, like an oasis in the middle of a parched desert, the book of Ruth adds elegance, grace, opulence and romance to an otherwise depressing situation.

It's in this exquisite book of romance, redemption and restoration that we'll find not only a powerful destiny-altering prayer but also destiny-altering decisions. I am referring particularly to those decisions we make that affect our future, the choices we live and die with.

Perhaps you have heard of the story of the guy named Fred. Fred had just inherited 10 million

> IT'S IN THIS EXQUISITE BOOK OF ROMANCE, REDEMPTION AND RESTORATION WE'LL FIND NOT ONLY A POWERFUL DESTINY ALTERING PRAYER BUT WE'LL ALSO FIND DESTINY ALTERING DECISIONS.

dollars, but the will stipulated that he had to accept the money in either Chile or Brazil. So Fred chose Brazil. Unfortunately, it turned out that in Chile he would have received his inheritance in the land on which Iranian gold and silver had just been discovered. But he made his choice. Once in Brazil, he had to choose between receiving his inheritance in coffee or in nuts. He chose the nuts. Too bad. The bottom fell out of the nut market, and coffee rose up $1.30 a pound wholesale unroasted. Poor Fred lost everything he had. He even had to sell his gold watch for the money he needed to fly back home.

It seemed that he had enough for a ticket to either New York or Boston. So Fred chose Boston. When the plane to New York taxied up, he noticed it was a brand new Boeing 747 with a red carpet and good-looking people and eye-popping stewardesses.

The plane to Boston arrived, and it was a 1928 Ford twin engine with a swayback, and it took a full day to get the plane off the ground. It was filled with crying babies and tethered goats.

Over the Andes Mountain, one of the twin engines fell out. And our man Fred made his way to the pilot and said, "I need to confess, I'm the jinx on this plane," much like Jonah did. He continued, "Let me out if you want to save your life. Give me a parachute." The pilot said "Okay, I'll do that. But on this plane, anybody who bails out has to wear two parachutes."

So Fred jumped out of the plane, and as he fell dizzily through the air, he tried to make up his mind which rip cord to pull. Finally, he chose the one on the left. It was rusty and the wire pulled loose. So then he pulled the other handle. The chute opened, but its shroud line snapped.

In desperation, Fred cried out to heaven, "St. Francis, save me!" And a hand grabbed the poor guy by the wrist and let him dangle in the air, and then a gentle but inquisitive voice said, "St. Francis of Xavier or St. Francis of Assisi?"

Destiny decisions! You may not have paid much attention to it, but there is a correlation between your destiny and your decisions. Chances are you have made some good decisions and some not-so-good decisions. So you know how important it is to make right decisions, be it a decision about who to marry, where to live, where to work—the list is endless.

Please understand, however bad the decisions are that you have made, I am not saying that God is not able to turn things around. I am not denying that you can rebuild your life again. God can take what is a mess and make a miracle out of it. He can turn your tests into your testimony, your tragedies into your triumphs. God can do all that and more in your life as He did for Ruth. But the point I am making is that your decision will still determine your destiny—good or bad!

Right away as we open to the Old Testament book of Ruth, in the first chapter we are confronted with a family making some big-time mistakes. We are confronted with a family that made some destiny-altering decisions that would later on have huge eternal consequences.

There are some decisions that can change your destiny and there are some decisions that can change your destiny to what it should be. Not what it *could* be, but what it *should* be. Do you know there is a difference between what could and what should? A lot of things that the Almighty God hasn't meant to be our destiny determinants can determine our destiny for us.

Allow me to show you from the first chapter of the book of Ruth two things that *could* determine your destiny. There are also two things that *should* determine your destiny.

Your Past

Your past can determine your destiny.

"Now it came about in the days when the judges governed" (Ruth 1:1). As you read this verse, right away you know that was bad news. The days when the judges governed was known as the Dark Ages in Hebrew history. It was a time of compromise, chaos and corruption. Sounds like our times, doesn't it? And to add insult to injury, verse 1 says there was a famine in Bethlehem. Don't miss that! *Bethlehem* means "house of bread." So there was no bread in Bethlehem because there was a famine in the land.

In verse 2 a man by the name of Elimelech, whose name means "my God is king," took a wife, Naomi, whose name means "pleasant," and they took their two sons to go sojourn in the land of

Moab. After some time in Moab, the two boys got
married to Moabite women. The name of one was
Orpah and the name of the other was Ruth.

Did you catch Ruth's past? First of all, she was
a Moabite. Who is a Moabite? Psalm 108 verse 9
says *"Moab is My
washbowl."* If you
know what a wash-
bowl is, you defi-
nitely don't want to
be called one. But
in the previous
verse, God called Judah His scepter. That's speak-
ing of somebody who rules, somebody who is the
head and not the tail. In sharp contrast, the Word
says Ruth was a washbowl. That was her past. In
other words, she was a nobody! And to add salt to
an injury that's already bad, Ruth lost her only
ticket to being a somebody when her Jewish husband died.

THE TRUTH BE TOLD, WHAT'S KEEPING SOME OF US FROM MOVING ON WITH OUR LIVES EVEN AFTER A BAD DECISION HAS BEEN MADE IS OUR OBSESSION WITH THE PAST.

What do you do when life deals you a lemon?
You do have a decision to make. You can sit and
keep sucking on your lemon or you can get back
up and starting making lemonade out of your
lemon. The truth be told, what's keeping some of
us from moving on with our lives even after a bad
decision has been made is our obsession with the
past. But here is an encouraging word from the
apostle Paul in Philippians 3:13 as you seek to
move past your past: *"[Forget] what lies behind and
[reach] forward to what lies ahead."* Meaning, don't
dig up dead stuff!

It's like the story I heard of a woman who happened to be looking out of her window one morning. She was horrified to see her German shepherd shaking the life out of her neighbour's rabbit. Her family had been quarrelling with this neighbour for a while, and the latest incident was certainly going to make matter worse. So she ran outside and yelled at her dog until he finally dropped the rabbit, now covered with dog spit and extremely dead.

After thinking what she should do, the woman lifted the rabbit and brought it into the house. She dumped the lifeless body of the rabbit into the bathtub and turned on the shower. She cleaned up the rabbit. Now she had a plan. She found her hair dryer and blew the rabbit dry, "Zzzzzz." Using an old comb, she groomed the rabbit until he looked pretty good. Then when the neighbour wasn't looking, she hopped over the fence, snuck across the backyard and propped the rabbit up in his cage. There was no way she was going to take the blame for Fluffy.

About an hour later, she heard a scream coming from her neighbour's yard. So she ran outside, pretending she didn't know what was going on. "What happened?" she asked innocently. Her neighbour came running to the fence, stunned, and said, "Our rabbit, our rabbit! He died two weeks ago. We buried him, and now he's back!"

Perhaps like that woman, you have been obsessed with what is dead and long buried. And all you can think of is how to bring the dead rabbit in your life back up again. No! Not Ruth! Ruth was determined to not let her past determine her destiny. Look at the destiny-altering decision she made after her mother-in-law Naomi tried to persuade her to go back to her past.

Then she said, "Behold, your sister-in-law has gone back to her people and her gods; return after your sister-in-law." But Ruth said, "Do not urge me to leave you or turn back from following you; for where you go, I will go, and where you lodge, I will lodge. Your people shall be my people, and your God, my God" (Ruth 1:15–16).

While we often hear this verse quoted at weddings by couples to each other, I chuckle, because this was a statement made by a daughter-in-law to her mother-in-law. More than that, this was a destiny-altering statement! It would be a decision that would change the trajectory of history, for Ruth and for us.

This brings me to the first thing that should determine your destiny.

Your God

Not your past, but your God! Why do I say your God should determine your destiny? Because your God is greater, your God is stronger and higher than your past! You know His name, don't you?

IN EVERY DECISION YOU MAKE YOU MUST TRUST GOD FOR THE STEPS AND THE RESULT.

He Is El Shaddai, the God of more than enough. If the book of Ruth teaches you anything, it is this: In

17

every decision you make you must trust God for the steps and the result.

Can I take you deeper? Contrast the decision Elimelech made by leaving Bethlehem for Moab with the decision Ruth made by clinging to Naomi and her God. When famine hit the land (Ruth 1:1) what did Elimelech do? As previously mentioned, Elimelech's name in Hebrew means "my God is king." What did "my God is king" do when famine hit the land?

"My God is king" acted like his God was no longer king. Could Elimelech have prayed and trusted God to provide for him even in Bethlehem, where there was no bread? I know a God who sent a raven to feed a prophet in a time of famine. David said, *"I have been young and now I am old, Yet I have not seen the righteous forsaken Or his descendants begging bread"* (Psalm 37:25). What I am saying is, even in uncertain times we need to know Jehovah-Jireh, the Lord our Provider.

Ruth said to Naomi, *"Your people shall be my people, and your God, my God."* She was not referring to her Moabite god, Chemosh. Don't miss that. What was Ruth's past? She was a washbowl. You remember? But now this Moabite woman is saying, "I want to be a Jewess." She refuses to be a washbowl any longer. It's time to let bygones be bygones. By choosing Yahweh God, Ruth was saying in essence, "Lord, let me be the apple of Your eye!"

Do you know what is so amazing about Ruth's decision? It happened! Ruth the washbowl, Ruth the Moabitess, was welcomed into the family of

God, even though the Bible said that couldn't happen. According to Deuteronomy it was against the law for a Moabite to be allowed into the assembly of Israel (Deuteronomy 23:3). But praise God, Ruth the Moabitess knew something in her spirit that most of us often forget when we are at a crossroad of decision. Although Ruth was an Old Testament saint, she knew what Romans 5:20 says: *"Where sin increased, grace abounded all the more."*

I encourage you to read the genealogy of Jesus Christ in Matthew 1, and there you will find Ruth in the list of the who's who of Jesus' ancestors. You may be wondering, how in the world did God take "a washbowl" and include her in the who's who list of Jesus' family? The answer is *grace*! Grace is God giving you what you don't deserve.

So, I don't know who you are reading this book, but God's message from His Word to you is that it doesn't matter what your past has been. It really doesn't matter if you have made 11 months of mistakes and bad decisions. Yes, you have blown it! You may have gone down some dead-end road that you shouldn't have, like Elimelech and Naomi, but the fact that you are reading this book suggests to me that there is hope. If you start clinging to your God today and you put your past under the blood, God will take you out of your Moab, out of your Lo-debar, and He'll turn your mistakes into your miracles when you decide to choose Him above all others.

But here is the game changer. You have to make a conscious decision that your past is your past and you won't go around digging up dead rabbit.

Your present

Your present is the second thing that could potentially determine your destiny. That's right! Your present circumstance is just as capable of preventing you from fulfilling your destiny as your past is. The present can just be as deceiving as the past.

Let me ask you, are the trials you are going through now going to go on forever? No! Your present trials too shall pass, in Jesus' name! Your present situation has not come to stay; this too shall pass. Someone was asked, "What's your favourite verse in the Bible?" And the person answered, "My favourite verse in the Bible is, 'And it came to pass.'"

I once counted how many times the phrase "And it came to pass" appeared in the Bible. I counted 396 times! That ought to make you want to shout for joy, because that tells me what you are going through now has not come to stay, but it too shall pass.

Just because your present circumstance has been troubling you for so long does not mean it's going to be forever. Sometimes God will display your problem for everyone to see so that when He delivers you, there will be no doubt as to who should get the glory.

Even Ruth's present was against her, not just her past. Her own mother-in-law, Naomi, told her to go back to Moab when God was leading Ruth to

Bethlehem, the house of bread. While Ruth was trying to make the right decision, her present circumstances seemed to be dictating otherwise.

Please understand, Satan can use even well-meaning people to keep your focus off your destiny. And there is no point getting mad at them. You are the one who has to make the decision. You get to make your own bed and lie in it. Just don't be like Adam, who shifted the blame: "Well, it's the woman you gave me; she made me do it." Instead, you've got to set your face like flint! Here was a woman who was convinced about what she wanted, and she was not going to let her past or her present stop her.

Three times in this text, Naomi told Ruth to go back to Moab (verses 8, 11 and 15), and each time Ruth said, "No, I am not going back!" Each time she was saying "No! No! No!" she was making the right choice, the right choice, the right choice. A lot of times we look at where a person ends up at the top without paying attention to the right choices they made to get them to where they are.

You ask, how in the world did Ruth maintain her resolve in the midst of conflicting voices? Imagine you are lined up in row with four other people. You can count who is first and second and third, etc., in line. Now, if all five of you in line turn around facing me, who will now be first in line? If my perspective is from the side, you are now all first! The point is, just because you didn't get started right in life, just because you were last on the list for promotion, just because you grew up in a dysfunctional home, just because your daddy didn't treat you right, doesn't mean you can't still have a wonderful life.

You are not too old! You can still go back to school. A middle-aged lady came to me the other day and said, "Pastor, guess what? I am going back to school." I said to her, "Go, girl; go, girl!" It's not too late to start that business. It's never too late to give that marriage or that son or daughter over to God.

Ruth was able to maintain her resolve because she understood that it's a dangerous thing to give up too soon. But whenever you decide to turn around from your original position, then you are turning in the direction of the second thing that should determine your destiny.

> RUTH WAS ABLE TO MAINTAIN HER RESOLVE BECAUSE SHE UNDERSTOOD THAT IT'S A DANGEROUS THING TO GIVE UP TOO SOON.

CHAPTER TWO

stay out of Moab

Your Decision Now

What you were before in line doesn't really matter anymore, because what you are now that you have turned around is what counts. You can't really do much about what's been done, but you can do something about what's done now. Ruth, whose name means "friendship," knew deep down in her spirit what the Bible says: "*Many who are first will be last, and many who are last will be first*" (Matthew 19:30, NIV).

So, don't let people count you out! You may have made some bad decisions, and you think you can't get to where you need to be anymore. Let Ruth tell you something: God will recalibrate the system and show you how to get to the place of your destiny, and you can make sound decisions and still get there. God is about to do something new and amazing in your life.

Just don't let your past hold you down; don't let your present deceive you either. Rather, hold on to your God. Be of good cheer! It is not over until you win! Let your prayer be "Lord, guard me from being obsessed with my past, and let me not be deceived by my present, but let me keep my eyes on You as Your will unfolds in my life." Amen!

Decide now, and get back on the road to Bethlehem.

I heard that a wise sage once said, "Life is like a roller coaster ride." If you have ever gone on a roller coaster ride, God bless you. I really don't like roller coaster rides. My family and I go to Six Flags Darien Lake every year. I used to enjoy the rides when I was much younger but not anymore. Call me chicken, call me whatever you want to call me, but you won't get me on a roller coaster ride.

There's something about those height-defying rides. It's all right going up, when the belts (wheels) are cranking up, but then you get to the top part. I would be okay right there if you just left me there. However the moment the ride starts going down, it's downhill for me. It just bothers me being a grown man crying for his momma. It's no fun for me. On the other hand, my children seems to be happy being terrified on the roller coaster. Not me!

There is something about those roller coaster rides. They look fun and exciting, moving fast, and all the while the music is playing, but whatever happens once you strap yourself in, you just have to deal with it. If you have lived long enough you'll know there are a few things in life that look thrilling, feel good, smell good or even taste good but are not necessarily good for you.

Sin is like a roller coaster ride. So what is it about this thrill, this rush like a roller coaster ride, this fascination with sin that causes people who profess faith in God to somehow still believe that sin is not as ugly as we say it is, somehow thinking one has to go into the world and taste whether or not sin is deadly?

The truth is, you don't have to try drugs to know they're ugly. Just look at what they do to people who are users. No, you don't have to go out to Moab to find out that you don't belong there. You don't have to live on the wild side to experience life. If there is one big detriment you need to watch for that can hinder your prayers, it is sin. David said, *"If I had cherished sin in my heart, the Lord would not have listened"* (Psalm 66:18, NIV).

IF THERE IS ONE BIG DETRIMENT YOU NEED TO WATCH FOR THAT CAN HINDER YOUR PRAYERS, IT IS SIN.

The first verse of Ruth chapter 1 says, *"There was a famine in the land. And a certain man of Bethlehem in Judah went to sojourn in the land of Moab with his wife and his two sons."* What is worse in this case is not that there was famine in the land. What was worse is that Elimelech ran off to Moab.

What's so ugly about Moab? Moab was a place that God had warned His people not to go to. Moab was a cursed place. In fact Deuteronomy

23:3 tells us that no Moabite would ever be allowed in the house of God.

Moab was a nation conceived in sin. Much like Egypt is a picture of bondage and Babylon a picture of captivity, Moab in the Bible is a picture of worldliness. Jeremiah 48:11 says, "*Moab hath been at ease from his youth, and he hath settled on his lees*" (KJV), meaning, he's been wallowing in his sin and still thinks it's all right.

Moab is a dangerous place to be in, regardless of whether there is a famine in Bethlehem or not. If you are a believer, being like this present world is not God's will for you. First John 2:15 says, "*Love not the world, neither the things that are in the world. If any man love the world, the love of the Father is not in him*" (KJV). Jesus says we are in the world but not of the world. We are not called to imitate the world, we are not called to be like the world, we are called to be world changers.

I know this chapter will be tough for a young person reading this book. We live in tough and perilous times. Hollywood is constantly pulling you away from God. MuchMusic, MTV and BET are constantly luring you away from God to Moab. But it's time for the body of Christ to stand up and take the other hand off the rope and start pushing the gates of hell back and say, "Devil! You can't have this generation of God's children. You can't have their minds; you can't have their bodies. Take your hands off God's property!"

I believe there is a great lesson that the Lord wants to teach us about staying out of Moab before we can experience the blessings of a Boaz prayer. What's astonishing to me in this first chapter is the trip to Moab that Elimelech took. Verses 3 and 5 say Elimelech and his two sons lost their lives while in Moab. They left Bethlehem, the house of bread, because of famine,

...THERE IS A GREAT LESSON THAT THE LORD WANTS TO TEACH US ABOUT STAYING OUT OF MOAB BEFORE WE CAN EXPERIENCE THE BLESSINGS OF A BOAZ PRAYER.

so they wouldn't die. But they ended up dead anyway. To be sure, they did not die because of hunger. The famine didn't kill them. There was plenty of food in Moab. But they died in Moab because the Bible says in Proverbs 14:12, "*There is a way that seems right to a man, but in the end it leads to death*" (NIV). Elimelech and his two sons fell simply because they found themselves in a deadly environment.

I have been pastoring for nearly two decades, and it's staggering to see young people as they begin to leave the house of God and their commitment to the Lord waning as they say, "I'm just going to take a trip to Moab and back. I'm just going to flirt with the world for a season." And then they fall! They don't get destroyed in Moab because the enemy is too strong for them. You won't fall because Satan's power is greater than God's power to keep you. There's no devil in hell that can pluck you out of God's hand! If you take a stand for God, the Bible guarantees God will take a stand for you. But I am saying that there are some places that you don't have any business going to as a believer. There are some websites that you shouldn't be going to if you are a believer. Do you understand that the Spirit of God that lives inside of you is not at all comfortable just being anywhere and everywhere? That's why when you are looking at a website you shouldn't be looking at and you are hanging out with people you shouldn't be with, you feel a nudging of the Spirit of God, saying, "You don't belong there. Get out of ——!"

Do you know why Elimelech left Bethlehem and went to Moab? Oh, he could have stayed in the house of bread and trusted God and prayed, "Give me this day our daily bread." But he went to Moab because Moab was enticing. Moab looked pretty with all its lights and sounds. That's why people go to Las Vegas! It is appealing to the flesh.

Satan will always make the sinful things of the world look wonderful. He will show you all the good times. It may look good and smell good. The grass may be greener on the other side, but it still has to be mowed!

Moab Disorients Its Victims

The first compelling reason you need to stay out of Moab is because Moab disorients its victims. Look at what it did to Elimelech and his family. They began to settle into their decision to go to Moab, which would later become hard to get out of.

In verse 1, it says they originally went to live in Moab *"for a while"* (NIV). The Hebrew word *sojourn* in verse 1 means to take a temporary residence.

But then in verse 2 the verb changes. It says *"they...remained there."* That's very significant. That means they moved from being temporary residents to being permanent residents in a land that God has told them to stay out of!

So now verse 4 tells us, *"they lived there about ten years,"* which says to me that they had no intention of returning to Bethlehem. But to further complicate the matter the text says the two sons got married to women from Moab, when God has said in His Word that He is not keen on His people hooking up with those who don't care about Him.

Can you see how slippery the slope gets? You cannot associate with the spirit of Moab and expect to not be burned. The reason God says to stay out of Moab is because Moab can destroy you. Not because God is a killjoy! Moab can hinder you.

Do you know how the Eskimos killed wolves? They would take a sharp knife and dip it in seals' blood. And they would hold it up and let it dry. Then they would dip it again and again until the knife basically a seals' blood popsicle. Then they would drive the handle of the blade into the snow.

A wolf can smell. He can smell blood from miles away. Seal is one of his favourite meals. And he'll come running, and he'll begin to lick that blade not knowing that there's danger, not knowing that he's licking something that can kill him. The crazy thing of it all is, this wolf is liking the blood of the seal on the knife but can't tell the difference between the seals' blood and his own blood, and his tongue is licking the sharp blade, and it's draining the very life out of him. It won't be long until he staggers off, weak and powerless. He is falling dead with blood gushing out of his mouth.

Though grotesque, that's what sin does to a man or woman. Moab looks attractive. The enemy wants to make you crave sin as a wolf craves seals' blood. But see, he doesn't show you the side of sin that can leave you weak and powerless. He doesn't show you the disaster that comes out of it. But what you need to know is, Moab disorients its victims!

Even strong young men and women can lose their way in Moab once they get there. And you know, the best way not to lose your way in Moab is not to go to Moab at all!

Let me tell you how Moab will get hold of you. Moab will get hold of your life first by controlling your mind, your thought life, what you think about. The enemy knows if he can get a stronghold in your mind, then he's got the whole of your life. That's why the Bible says in Proverbs 23:7, "*For as [a man] thinketh in his heart, so is he*" (KJV). Or as Joyce Meyers would say, "Where the mind goes, the man follows."

THE BEST WAY NOT TO LOSE YOUR WAY IN MOAB IS NOT TO GO TO MOAB AT ALL!

You can't be listening to Shakira and Eminem and P. Diddy and Lady Gaga and not have your mind polluted. It's garbage in, garbage out. There was a time in my life when I was watching a soap opera. I got hooked on it, and before I knew it I

DR. TAI A. ADEBOBOYE

started thinking like Jack on *All My Children*. For you it's *Jersey Shore!* You keep clicking on that mouse, visiting that filthy website, and you're saying to yourself, "But it's not hurting anyone!" You'd better get rid of the mouse! Otherwise sin will trap you in Moab.

Here's what I want you to see: Moab got hold of Elimelech before he knew it! You may be messing around with a little sin right now, and you're thinking it won't hurt you. No! Don't be deceived.

I heard about a circus show in Italy that went tragically wrong. There was this man, and one of his acts involved bringing a huge python into the ring, and this python would wrap itself around him. He would stand up straight like a stick, and this python would wrap itself around him so all you could see was a column of snake. (The audience sitting in the circus would probably be feeling the hairs on the back of their necks standing up as they watched this creepy thing.) Then the guy would give a signal. He had trained the python, and the python would slowly release itself around the man and slither across the ring. Everybody would break into applause. It was the grand crescendo of the performance.

It was the same performance one day. The guy stood ramrod, and the python wrapped itself around him. The audience sat there; it was absolute silence as they watched. Then suddenly, there was a loud crack and then a scream. Some of the circus workers quickly ran into the ring, realizing what had happened. They actually had to kill the snake, but not before the python had constricted and crushed the guy and killed him.

Later, it was revealed that this man had gotten the python when it was just newly hatched in Africa and kept it with him. It slept in his pocket; he took it in to his bed. Everywhere he went, he took this python, so that the python grew up thinking this man was his parent—just an odd-shaped python with two legs and two arms, that's all.

A snake is still a snake, isn't it?

When he got that python, this little baby, just a couple of feet long when it was hatched, the guy could have taken its head between his thumb and finger and crushed its head just like that! But he didn't. He just played with it, sought to train it. As the python grew bigger, the man could have crushed it with his thumbs had he wanted to. Later it turned around to be the one crushing him.

When I heard that story I said, "What a picture of sin!" It starts little, and we think it won't hurt us. We even think we can't resist it, and we begin to push the boundaries a little bit here and there—until it crushes us! Forgive me if I am being too graphic here. You know why I am not holding back? I see a lot of Christians today flirting with sin. I'm seeing what Moab is doing to many lives, ruining many destinies, so that *"There is a way which seems right to a man, But its end is the way of death"* (Proverbs 14:12).

So if I am excessive, pardon me, but somebody needs to stand up and call sin—sin! Don't let's call it what it isn't. "Oh, she's dysfunctional!" "That's the way she was born!"

Let's quit sugar-coating sin. We've got to let our young people know that Moab is a deadly place to be in! Parents, you can't just sit back and watch what your kids are doing these days. If you do, they will be too far gone before you know it. No! You've got to be involved in their lives and tell them what's right and what's wrong. Why? Because you've been there and they have not!

It seems to me that the problem with temptation is curiosity. And the problem with curiosity is the idea that somehow this will be different from that. No! *"There is nothing new under the sun"* said King Solomon (Ecclesiastes 1:9). *"Vanity of vanities! All is vanity"* (Ecclesiastes 1:2).

Every now and then my kids and I would talk about something that they wanted to do that was outside the boundaries of our family. And I'd say, "No!" And my kids would say, "But everybody else is doing it." And I'd say, "But we are not everybody else! We are the Adeboboyes, sons and daughters of the Most High God!"

I know the peer pressure on our young people is greater than anything we grown-ups have ever known. But I also believe with all my heart that by God's grace you can also be a Daniel. You can be an Esther, you can be a Ruth, you can be different—not weird, but different for Jesus! This generation needs you all to be different!

Moab Disconnects Its Victims

The second reason why you need to stay out of Moab is because Moab disconnects its victims. See, the land of Moab for you might be a thoughtful, handsome guy or that hot girl in school or at your workplace who makes you feel very warm inside. But he or she doesn't trust in Jesus Christ and doesn't live for your God.

When you choose to date that girl or guy who is not a Christian, know this for sure: you've chosen that person over Jesus. I know what you're saying. "But Dr. Tai, if I go out with him, I'll witness to him, and I'd invite him to come with me to church. He'll change." No, you don't know that for sure! Ninety-nine percent of the time you'll be the one who ends up turning away from God! That's why the Bible says, "*Do not be unequally yoked together with unbelievers*" (2 Corinthians 6:14, NKJV).

Can you see how Moab turned Elimelech, whose name means "God is my king"? Can you see how Moab turned "God is my king" away from his God? It turned him away

MOAB WILL DISCONNECT YOU FROM THE PROTECTION OF GOD.

to a point of no return. That's what Moab does! Moab will disconnect you from the protection of God. Once you leave Bethlehem, the house of bread, for Moab, you are on your own. Where God has an obligation to provide and protect you is in Bethlehem, not in Moab, a cursed place!

Listen to Naomi's understanding of all that happened to her and her husband and two sons: "*For the hand of the LORD has gone forth against me*" (verse 13) and "*I went out full, but the LORD has brought me back empty. Why do you call me Naomi, since the LORD has witnessed against me and the Almighty has afflicted me?"* (verse 21). Witnessed about what? She is saying that God was not obligated to bless her in Moab.

Battling Satan on the side of Bethlehem is easier than battling Satan on the side of Moab, because when you're standing where God wants you to be and living right, you are on the Lord's side. And when you call on the name of Jesus, every demon has to run from you. Whenever you say "It is written!" every demon has to bow at the name of Jesus.

So you see it's easier to battle on the Lord's side, because you're connected to power from on high, than it is to battle in Moab. When you're in Moab and the demons are attacking you and you say, "Oh, in the name of Jesus go away!" they'll laugh at you and they'll say, *"Jesus I know, and Paul I know; but who are you?"* (Acts 19:15, NKJV). You are on their turf. And they might very well turn around and beat you up as they did the seven sons of Sceva!

That's why the devil tries to keep you disconnected in Moab.

But the good news is that God's obligated to bless you in the promised land! Because God has sworn, *"I will bless him, and will make him fruitful and will multiply him exceedingly"* (Genesis 17:20). In Jesus' name you will get to your promised land! You may not get to your destiny as quickly as you want to, but in the mighty name of Jesus, you'll get there.

Look how beautiful chapter 1 of the book of Ruth ends: "*So Naomi returned, and with her Ruth the Moabitess*" (verse 22). I love that! "*So Naomi returned, and with her Ruth.*" Ruth stayed out of Moab and came to Bethlehem!

She is now ready for the next phase of her life. Ruth is now ready for the Boaz prayer to be prayed over her life, now that she refuses to let her past determine her future and now that she has stayed clear from what could hinder her prayer—Moab.

The good news for you too is that it doesn't matter how far you've gone into Moab. From this moment on you can return to Jesus! Do you understand that Jesus came and died to bring you out of Moab? The Father sent His Son to die for your sins on the cross. They drove nails into His hands and feet so that you wouldn't have to suffer. Jesus died so that you wouldn't have to die in Moab. He was crucified to set you free! He is calling you to the foot of His cross. When you come to Jesus He doesn't subtract from you. His cross is a plus sign. He adds to your life. So get ready for the blessings of the Boaz prayer.

> RUTH IS NOW READY FOR THE BOAZ PRAYER TO BE PRAYED OVER HER LIFE, NOW THAT SHE REFUSES TO LET HER PAST DETERMINE HER FUTURE AND NOW THAT SHE HAS STAYED CLEAR FROM WHAT COULD HINDER HER PRAYER—MOAB.

CHAPTER THREE

The favour factor

"May the LORD reward your work, and your wages be full from the LORD, the God of Israel, under whose wings you have come to seek refuge" (Ruth 2:12).

Four expectant fathers were pacing up and down in a hospital waiting room while their wives were in labour. This was in the days when men were not allowed in the delivery room. One of the nurses came out and told the first man, "Congratulations, you're the father of twins; your wife just gave birth to twins."

What a coincidence!" the man replied, "I work for the Minnesota Twins baseball team."

A little while later, the nurse returned and told the second man, "Congratulations, you're the father of triplets!"

"That's really an incredible coincidence," he answered. "I work for 3M Corporation."

An hour later, the nurse told the third man that

his wife had just given birth to quadruplets. The man with the sound of disbelief in his voice said, "I don't believe it! I work for the Four Seasons hotels. What a coincidence!"

After hearing this, everyone's attention turned to the fourth guy, who had just fainted. He slowly regained consciousness and then whispered, "I should never have taken that job at The Fifth Estate!"

When things happen that defy our expectations, the world calls it a coincidence. Coincidence is anything that happens by chance. Some people call it luck, and they put a lot of hope in getting lucky! That's why you always get stuck in line paying for gas behind someone buying Lotto Max Jackpot tickets. Have you noticed that we live in a culture that strongly believes in lucky breaks?

But the Bible doesn't talk at all about luck or getting lucky. That's a word you've got to quit using. Instead, what the world calls coincidence, what the people of this present age call lucky breaks, the Bible calls favour!

Coincidence is anything that happens to you by chance. But favour is God working on your behalf even if you don't deserve it. When something unusual happens in your life, how actively involved you believe God is in your life will

WHEN SOMETHING UNUSUAL HAPPENS IN YOUR LIFE, HOW ACTIVELY INVOLVED YOU BELIEVE GOD IS IN YOUR LIFE WILL DETERMINE WHETHER YOU SEE THAT EVENT AS A MERE COINCIDENCE OR YOU SEE IT AS GOD'S FAVOUR.

determine whether you see that event as a mere coincidence or you see it as God's favour.

As we come to chapter 2 of Ruth, what the Bible wants you to understand is, once you start to walk in God's way, you don't need to carry chicken's feet in your purse or wallet hoping some lucky breaks will come your way, as Madame Hocus Pocus told you to. No, once you become righteous, once you turn around in the direction God told you to turn, my Bible says in Psalm 37:23–24, "*The steps of a good man are ordered by the LORD, And He delights in his way. Though he fall, he shall not be utterly cast down*" (NKJV).

That's favour! Though you're down, the Bible says, you won't be counted out by God, because His favour that reaches down to grab you out of Moab will lead you back to Bethlehem—the house of bread, where what didn't work for you before will begin to work for you.

Some of you reading this book can testify to what I'm talking about here. Folks thought you were down and out, but God's love lifted you. What killed other people you knew in Moab only gave you a wake-up call, and now you are alive to talk about it. "*If the LORD had not been on our side…they would have swallowed us alive… Praise be to the LORD, who has not let us be torn*" (Psalm 124:1-6, NIV).

If you have been to Moab and back, aren't you glad you came out of Moab alive? Or maybe I should call up Ruth and Naomi to come and testify to you. Our text says, "*So Naomi returned*" (Ruth 1:22). So Naomi—not Naomi and Elimelech and their two boys—returned. Let that sink in. Rather, Naomi returned and with her Ruth the Moabitess. What other folks couldn't survive from their trip to Moab, Ruth and Naomi survived!

What AIDS did to other people who were sleeping around, what HIV did to other folks who were shooting up drugs, what liver cirrhosis did to other people who were alcoholics, did not kill you. You came out unscathed, and you are alive to talk about it. What killed others, the cancer that took other people's lives, left you with only a scar. And you're still talking about coincidence and getting a lucky break? If that's not the favour of God in your life, as it was for Ruth and Naomi, then I have nothing else to say to you. But if you understand that it is God's favour that has kept you alive till this day, then you ought to take a moment and give God the praise that is due Him!

Oh! I know favour ain't fair! But who says favour is fair?

And God wasn't finished with Ruth and Naomi yet. Ruth 2:1 says, *"Now Naomi had a kinsman of her husband."* Oh! She had a what? So she still had something. I thought she said earlier, "I *went out full, but the LORD has brought me back empty."* She thought all hope was lost. But the Lord is about to show her she still has something. She has a kins-man of her husband, but not just an ordinary kins-man. She has a wealthy kinsman, whose name is Boaz. *Boaz* in Hebrew means "strength."

Then Ruth the Moabitess said to Naomi, *"Please let me go to the field and glean among the ears*

40

of grain after one in whose sight I may find favor"
(Ruth 2:2). She didn't say whose field.
Nevertheless, this request of Ruth's for favour is
the beginning of the Boaz prayer I want to introduce you to. I pray favour over you as you are
about to enter a new season of supernatural blessings like Ruth.

Right from this text, let me begin to share with
you four factors the favour of God will do for you
as you begin to include the Boaz prayer in your
daily prayers.

#1 God's favour will bring you to the right place

There were many fields that Ruth could have
gone to glean in that morning. But *"she happened
to come to the portion of the field belonging to Boaz,
who was of the family of Elimelech"* (Ruth 2:3). You
remember who Elimelech was, don't you?
Elimelech was a relative of Boaz, whose field
Ruth "happened" on. The text says Ruth just
"happened to come to." The King James translation
says *"and her hap was to light on a part of the field
belonging unto Boaz."*

Wait a minute. This was no happenstance! This
was no lucky break! This ain't coincidence. At least,
that's not what the Bible is saying here. This was Ruth
finding what she was praying for in verse 2. This was
divine favour bringing Ruth to the right place!

I want you to think with me for a moment
about the unlikelihood of this being a coincidence
or lucky break.

For Ruth to "happen" upon the field of Boaz is very high odds, almost an impossibility. Talk about being in the right place at the right time—this is it!

As Ruth was going out that morning, it was very important that she get in the right field, because your future and my future was dependent upon it. You say, how? If she hadn't, then there wouldn't have been a Christmas. You will understand the implication of this first prayer of being at the right place later on as we get to the final chapter of the book.

It was critical that Ruth should go into the right field. How could she, without a map or GPS? When Marian and I went to Bethlehem in Israel for our 20th anniversary, we saw hundreds of fields in the countryside. And back in ancient times (and even now) they didn't have fences around the fields; there weren't even paths in between. What you would see is one field running into another field. Certainly, there wasn't a sign out saying "This is Boaz's field, visitors welcome!" I mean, you wouldn't even know whose field you were in unless you happened to be the owner or you worked there. But the Bible says Ruth just went out and happened to come to *the* place, not just any place.

Let me tell you something about the place. Everything in Ruth's life up until this point was on a continuous downward spiral—until she came to the place. She was a young woman. She had lost her husband and left her home, which she knew very well. Now she was poor, frustrated and confused.

Have you ever been poor? What a dumb question to ask! Ever been frustrated and confused like Ruth, in a country where you are not particularly welcome? Of course the question is *not* if God can bless in any given situation. God was blessing His people mightily again in Bethlehem, as Ruth 1:6 tells us. The question is, can God bless a woman whose has been through hell and high water? Can God bless you, a jobless person, and bring you to the right place, the field of your dreams? Can God take you, an employee, and make you become the employer? Can the Almighty God bring you to the right place?

Don't let the enemy intimidate you. Don't let a new place push you back to Moab. You've been through too much agony in Moab already to be intimidated. The reason you're now back in Bethlehem (Naomi) is that you are about to see the favour of God in your life that will rock your world! The Bible says Ruth *"happened to come to the portion of the field belonging to Boaz,"* a relative! That's the favour factor for you right there. She didn't just stumble into any field. No! Her steps were ordered by the Lord to happen upon the right field!

Perhaps you took a chance of leaving a place that you knew so well and you came to an intimidating place where nobody knew you. Now you have to start all over again. The fact is, when God begins to order your steps, sometimes you have to go to someplace where you are a foreigner, where you will look like a "Moabitess," where you will look like you never owned anything to your name.

Several years ago I left Lagos, Nigeria, my home in Africa. I was a great leader in my little church in Lagos. There I was "the man." I was teaching and preaching, leading people to Jesus. Then I found myself in Toronto, where nobody knew me. I came with only one suit. I didn't even have a winter coat in a cold January. I had on a suit named after two women, Poly and Ester. I was intimidated! I was a few inches shorter than I am now and fifty pounds lighter. Oh! I was blown around in Toronto. There were times I wondered, "Oh my God, what am I doing here in this cold country?" I had no money and nothing I could call my own. But God had other plans for me, because the only way He could take me to the right place of my destiny was to bring me out of my comfort zone.

Today, praise God, I can tell you that I have been blessed beyond measure! Not lucky, but blessed! As I look back, no doubt God was ordering my steps. Before I left Nigeria, one of my prayers was for the Lord to lead me to the right place of my destiny. I had two choices of where to immigrate to, Canada or the U.S. I thank God He brought me to the right place, because being in the right place was going to bring me to the right person of my dreams!

Maybe you too are not where you are right now by accident. It's no fluke. There's a reason that you're where you are. God is the one who has been behind the curtain like a puppet master pulling strings in your life to bring you to the right place. Sorry, no offence; it's not that you were smart enough to know where to go, it's not that you're great, it's not that you're good—but God's favour found you and pointed you in the right direction and released you into your destiny, and now you're in your Bethlehem.

On the other hand, if you feel like you are in the middle of a place called "nowhere," like Ruth once was, this moment could be your divine appointment to begin praying for the Lord to bring you to the right place He has in store for you. For you perhaps the right place of your destiny is not a new country but a new job. You have been in that dead-end job for so long, and now is the time for the change you have been longing for.

prayer guide

Why not begin to pray daily for the Lord to order your steps to the right place of employment, as Ruth did? It could be an opportunity to enter a new business arena you need to pray over or a new area of ministry where you can serve God more effectively. Wherever the right place is for you, begin to believe that with God all things are possible.

#2. god's favour will bring you to the right person

What you need to understand next is that there is a correlation between getting to the right place at the right time and meeting the right person of your dreams. One sure way of knowing that you have come to the right place is that doors will also open for you to meet the right person—your Boaz.

That's what the next favour factor will do for you as you pray the Boaz prayer.

The miracle of this story is that Ruth not only happened into the right place at the right time, but she also happened to the right person—Boaz, the one who owned the field Ruth came to.

The text says in verse 4 that Boaz happened to have left Bethlehem and he happened to be coming out of the city to visit the field that day. And he happened to be looking in Ruth's direction when she happened to be at the right place (verse 5). The implication is that had she happened on that place any other time, she would have missed her miracle. But because she was in the right place at the right time, time and destiny kissed each other and she met the right person of her dreams.

So Boaz came to his field that morning. There could have been several hundred girls gleaning in that field, and verse 5 says, "*Boaz asked the foreman of his harvesters, 'Whose young woman is that?'*" (NIV). "Who is that hot chick?" (that's my translation). The King James translation says, "*Whose damsel is this?*" Mmm mm! Ruth must have been a really pretty woman. You can't see that in the text, but that's what is implied here. Do you know what Ruth's name means? *Ruth* means "beauty." And believe me, Ruth's momma wouldn't have named her Beauty if she wasn't beautiful. Names had meaning back then. It's not like today when people name their children Rocket or Blanket.

Boaz then, whose name means "strength," met Ruth, whose name means "beauty." Strength and

Beauty met. Place and Person kissed each other for Beauty and Strength to meet. And I tell you, when Strength and Beauty meet, watch out now!

When I met my wife, Marian, she was from Cambridge, Ontario, and I was from Lagos, Nigeria, and the chances of knowing and befriending each other were very remote. There was no Facebook 21 years ago, no eHarmony.com either. But while I was in seminary I was a student pastor at a church downtown. And Marian moved from Cambridge to start a job downtown.

I was minding my own business, serving on the platform that morning, asking people to greet each other. I looked to my left at the congregation, and my eyes caught this young damsel, and I was like "Mmm mm! Who is this hot chick?" She was a hot chick then; she still is now. Thank God for greeting time in our churches. So I quickly told the people to move around and greet one another.

Immediately I ran off the platform and dashed toward where Marian was sitting. People thought I had to go the bathroom, but no, I wanted to get to Marian before any other eligible bachelor got to her first. I introduced myself to her. "Hi, my name is Tai, like *tie*. Do I know you from somewhere?" That was the line back then. The rest is history 20-plus years later! But see, you can call meeting the person of your dreams a coincidence or karma. I call it "the favour factor!"

Let me tell you something else. Six years ago when I went back to Nigeria to bury my dad, I was sitting in our living room in Lagos, and I looked up to the ceiling and noticed this little cut-out picture of a cherub still hanging down from the ceiling. As a little boy I used to look up to that cherub. Whenever we were doing our family prayer time in the morning, I'd be staring at the cherub. So, six years ago the cherub was still hanging, and it caught my attention. I noticed for the very first time that that cherub had red hair and freckles on her face. Stay with me now. A redheaded cherub in Africa? You figure that one out! Suddenly it dawned on me that even before I met Marian, God was already ordering my steps so that I would come to the right place at the right time and destiny and time would kiss each other for me to meet the woman of my dreams—my angel, who I have been staring at for years. By the way, my wife Marian has red hair, and she has freckles too when she is mad at me.

You may think you just "happened" to pick this book up. No! This is a setup. You are in the right place at the right time to receive the right message for what you are going through at this crucial junction of your life. God can lead you to the right person! He brought Eve to Adam (Genesis 2:22). He did it for Isaac and Rebecca, just as He brought Marian to me. And here He brought Ruth to Boaz. He can do it for you too. What God did 3,000 years ago He still does today.

God is about to raise up a Boaz in your life who will go out of his way to give you a hand to get that business off the ground. Yes! He has a blessing with your name written on it. Only believe and pray for Him to send your Boaz to you.

What I find intriguing is, of all the fields in all the places Ruth could have gone to, she ended up in Boaz's field. Does that sound like a lucky break to you? And of all the women gleaning in that field, Ruth was the one Boaz "happened" to take notice of. Don't sell me that coincidence stuff, because I am not buying it! This is nothing but favour!

Use your sanctified imagination to picture this with me. There could have been close to 200 women in that field that day. And Boaz came, riding on his donkey. All the Jewish girls there were giggling among themselves, saying, "He's coming down, he is coming down." They all knew he was an eligible bachelor. Each one of them could very well think he was coming for her.

Then he passed the first girl. Then the second girl said, "Oh, it's me he's coming for!" He passed her too. Then he passed the third. The fourth was sure Boaz was coming for her. On and on he passed them until he came to where Ruth was, and all the girls were muttering underneath their breath, "It cannot be her. It cannot be that Moabitess woman from Moab." So the last Jewish girl standing did all she could to make Boaz notice her. She turned around, and Boaz was gone. Not you too, baby!

So Boaz passed by everyone, and he took notice of only Ruth, and he said, "*Listen carefully, my daughter*" (Ruth 2:8). My what? That's favour coming! Do you understand that if the favour of God is upon you people are going to love you who have no business loving you? You can be working next to somebody at your workplace right now who is going to bless you, and he can't help himself. I declare and pray the Boaz prayer over you right now that God will raise up that person, your Boaz, who is going to "notice" you.

Did you realize again that Ruth was a Moabitess? Even the foreman who worked for Boaz seemed to be hammering the fact, as if to say, "Boaz, you don't want her; that is Ruth, the woman from Moab" (see Ruth 2:6). But what Mr. Foreman needed to understand is that the favour of God and the love of God, as the old hymn says, is greater than tongue or pen can ever tell. It goes beyond the highest star and reaches to the lowest hell. Hallelujah!

As I close this chapter, whoever you are reading this book, I want to say to you again, it doesn't matter what your past is. It doesn't matter where you came from or who your daddy is. It doesn't even matter what the colour of your skin is. What matters is, God's favour will lift you up from the ashes of your past, and it will seat you among the princes of His people (Psalm 113:7–9). His favour will bring you to the right person of your dreams. Whom God has blessed no man can curse!

prayer guide

Simply ask God to begin preparing your Boaz to meet you and take notice of you.

CHAPTER FOUR

The favour factor ain't over

Aren't you glad that you are surrounded by God's love? Everywhere you go, His love is all around you. I know you think it's the Elizabeth Taylor perfume or that Hugo Boss cologne you are wearing that is making you so irresistible to your suitors. But let the truth be told: no perfume or cologne makes you more desirable. It's the favour of God drawing people to you all this time, and you didn't even know it.

At the end of Ruth chapter 1 we see Ruth and Naomi returning from Moab because there was no way they were going to stay in Moab. To stay in Moab meant death!

Remember, Moab is a picture of worldliness. Moab is everything that stands against God's will for your life. So if by divine providence you are reading this book and you are still stuck in your own Moab but you want out, then it's time you kiss your Moab goodbye. God's plan is not for you to die in Moab. Come what may, you've got to be determined to get out of Moab, because God has something nice ready for you in Bethlehem, the house of bread.

The quandary I have with the church is that we keep preaching and telling people who are in Moab to come out of Moab but we don't tell them enough of what the alternatives are to Moab. The church talks more about hell and what's in hell than we talk about heaven and what's in heaven waiting for us. Whatever happened to letting people know that when God tells them to stay out of Moab it is because He has favour waiting for them in Bethlehem? That's why chapter 2 of Ruth is oozing with favour at the heels of chapter 1. You can't leave hell to follow God and get back into hell again if you are truly following God. If you can, then why has He saved you from hell? I am not implying that you won't have trials after you fully surrender your life to the Lord. But, praise God, Proverbs 12:2 says, "*A good man will obtain favor from the LORD.*"

So as Ruth returned to Bethlehem, God's favour started to cause three factors to happen in her life. First, God's favour brought her to the right place. You remember where favour brought Ruth? To the right field! Not just any field. There were hundreds of field she could have stumble into that day, but "*she happened to come to the portion of the field belonging to Boaz*" (Ruth 2:3). It was not happenstance. It was not a lucky break that brought her there. What brought her there was favour!

Second, God's favour brought her to the right person. The right person for Ruth was Boaz. There could have been around 200 maidens on the field that morning. But because Ruth was at the right place at the right time, time and destiny kissed each other to bring Ruth to the right person—Boaz.

Thus all that the Lord brought to Ruth since she came out of Moab was good. But the favour factor ain't over yet. There is a third favour factor.

#3. God's favour will bring you the right provision

From verses 8 to 16 of Ruth chapter 2 there is nothing but more favour after favour. I couldn't help but notice how Boaz treated Ruth and all that he did for her. If what was recorded in those verses isn't favour, then I don't know what favour is. I mean, this is unreal. We are talking about a Moabitess being treated like a queen. Remember, she is from Moab. Her past labeled her as a washbowl, a nobody, and now she was being treated like a princess.

Boaz was literally telling Ruth not to work. He told the reapers not to take everything out of the field. So they started dropping grain purposefully for her (Ruth 2:16). As Ruth started coming behind, gleaning, she started getting those unnatural blessings. Things that she couldn't even explain had been left lying on the ground for her. When God's favour finds you too, you will start seeing blessings drop into your lap that won't even make sense to you. You won't even be the next person in line for the promotion and the promotion will come to you.

After Ruth responded to Boaz in Ruth 2:10, and after Boaz told Ruth not to go anywhere else but to stay in his field and that she was now welcome around the water cooler with the rest of the Jewish girls, look at what else Boaz did for this woman. Look at what more provision the favour factor of God brought her. *"At mealtime Boaz said to her, 'Come here, that you may eat of the bread [meaning no more breadcrumbs along the trail] and dip your piece of bread in the vinegar.' So she sat beside the reapers"* (Ruth 2:14). Now, it's no more just around the water cooler that she's welcome; now she is allowed into the diner.

And on top of that, guess who served her? Boaz served her! Who was the boss? I thought Boaz was the boss. I thought Boaz owned the field. So who should be serving who? Don't miss what the Bible says. *"He served her roasted grain, and she ate and was satisfied and had some left"* (verse 14). Can you see what the favour of God can do in a life?

It should not surprise you that when you start to seriously walk with God— and I am not talking about only going to church on Sundays, but I mean when you truly surrender your life and your dreams to God as Ruth did—then God is obligated to take care of you. I remember when I was attending seminary, people would just walk up to me and say, "Tai, the Lord laid you on my heart." Have you ever had that said to you before? And you get one of those holy handshakes that has a cheque in it! I love those holy handshakes with something in them that comes at the right time. How did that person know I needed the blessings right at that moment? It was the favour of God bringing the right provision! Yes, He will do it for you too at the right time, at the right place, with the right person. Suddenly a refund cheque you had forgotten, just enough to get you through what you are going through, will drop on your lap, and you'll sing "Praise God from whom all blessings flow."

One of my good friends in my church, Neil Morgan, has been praying the Boaz prayer. He recently testified about receiving a call from the car dealership saying that he had overpaid them when he was purchasing his new vehicle. He thought they were refunding him only a couple of dollars, but to his surprise he was issued a cheque for couple of thousand dollars.

Can you imagine how happy Ruth was, coming out of her despicable conditions in Moab, to now see wheat and favour dropping on her left, right and centre? That is why I have often taught people not to be intimidated by the naysayers when they are praising God. Your naysayers do not know what life was like for you in Moab. They have no idea where you came from to get to where you are now. So when you are praising the Lord, it is because you are thankful for His favour in your life. Maybe people around you are used to eating wheat for breakfast. But you are not used to all these blessings around you. God brought you a mighty long way, from your spiritual Moab. Yes! He did you a favour, and that's why you cannot help but praise Him like you are doing. That's what He did for

Ruth. That's what He did for the church. He did us a favour!

It's true as it has often been said, "Favour ain't fair." It's not fair that Ruth received all these provisions that other women had to work for. But who says favour is fair anyway? Remember, favour is God working out on your behalf even if you are undeserving. That sounds like grace to me. Sometimes God can shower His goodness on you through people who don't even like you. He will even use people who can't stand you to bless you because they won't be able to resist you.

You may have heard the story of this Christian lady who lived next door to an atheist. Every day when the lady prayed, the atheist could hear her. And he would say to himself, "It is that crazy woman praying again. Doesn't she know there is no God?" Often she would be praising the Lord, and the atheist guy would go over to harass her, saying, "Lady, quit it! Don't you know there is no God?" But the lady would keep praying; she would keep praising.

One day this Christian lady ran out of groceries. As usual she was praying to the Lord, explaining her situation and thanking God for what He was going to provide. As usual too, the atheist heard her praying and thought to himself, "Hmm! I'll fix her!" So he went to the grocery store, bought a whole bunch of groceries, took them to the Christian lady's house and dropped them off on the front porch. He rang the doorbell and hid behind the bushes to see what she would do.

When she opened the door and saw the groceries, she began to praise the Lord with all her heart, jumping, singing and shouting. The atheist then jumped out of the bushes and said, "You crazy old lady. God didn't buy you those groceries. I told you there was no God!"

The Christian lady, hearing that, broke out and started running down the street, shouting some more and praising the Lord. The atheist ran after her. When he finally caught up to her, he asked, "What is the problem with you, lady? Didn't you hear me say I provided you with the groceries?"

The woman, still trying to catch her breath, looked the atheist in the eye and said, "I knew the Lord would provide me with some groceries, but I didn't know He was going to make the devil pay for them!" The Lord may even use people who can't stand you to bring the provision to you.

I know the world may call an uncanny blessing coincidence, but I don't believe in lucky breaks or happenstance. Instead I call it the favour factor! Even when God gives me a parking spot at a busy mall around Christmas, I say "Thank You, Lord, for Your favour, for Your provision."

Can you just see all the other ladies turning their noses up at Ruth, being snooty, saying, "What is she doing here? Why is she here?" And Boaz said, "Ruth, why don't you come and eat with us?" But she didn't just come to the table; Boaz himself served her! What was David's declaration in Psalm 23:1? *"The LORD is my shepherd, I shall not want."* He continued in verse 5, "*You prepare a table before me in the presence of my enemies; You have anointed my head with oil; My cup overflows.*" I pray and declare it over you, your cup is getting ready to overflow with God's favour too, in Jesus' name.

The text says Boaz served the food to Ruth personally so no one would doubt that she belonged there. And the Bible said she was given more than she needed. "*She also took it out and gave Naomi what she had left after she was satisfied*" (Ruth 2:18). And Naomi said, "Where did you get this from, girl?" (see verse 19). She said, "I was gleaning out in the field, and God's favour brought me to this nice guy, and he told his men to leave a handful on purpose for me, and I kept some and brought it." Naomi enquired, "What's the man's name?" And sheepishly Ruth said, "Boaz." "Oh, Boaz!" exclaimed Naomi. "He is my husband's relative. Yeah, he is related!" And Ruth stood there somewhat in disbelief.

But God was not finished with Ruth yet. Naomi knew the barley and wheat harvests would soon be over, and now was the time to get proactive about these two lovebirds getting married. If Boaz treated those who gleaned on his field this nicely, there was no telling what he would do as a husband.

More and more in my own life and ministry I am experiencing God as the God of the "suddenly." If God Almighty is your God, that means your life can take a sudden turn in a moment. Things can turn around 180 degrees out of nowhere. It could be one phone call, one meeting, one new opening, and your whole life will change. This could very well be your "suddenly" season.

Several years ago I was praying this aspect of the Boaz prayer, for God to bring me to the right person with the right provision who would go out of his way to help me. Then an opportunity came for me to have a TV ministry. I had always desired to expand my ministry to include reaching people through the airwaves. But I couldn't afford it. Before a fall conference at my church the Lord laid it on my heart to invite Reverend Norm MacLaren, who was one of the co-hosts on *100 Huntley Street*, to be our guest speaker at the conference. Later on the Lord would use Norm MacLaren, Paul Willoughby and the CTS ministry to be my "Boaz" in making room for me to begin a TV ministry on the Crossroads Television System (CTS) as co-host on *Nite Lite*, a ministry that was not only a blessing to me but brought hope and deliverance to a lot of troubled hearts in the dark night of their souls. For nearly two years, God provided this TV ministry for me at no expense. I considered that God's favour, bringing me to the right provision.

Here, God's favour is about to move Ruth from being an employee to being an employer. She is about to move from being a gleaner on the field to an owner of the field. That's what the right provision from God can do for you, as Solomon noted in Proverbs 10:22: "*It is the blessing of the LORD that makes rich, And He adds no sorrow to it.*"

prayer Guide

The Lord has promised to supply all our needs according to His riches in Christ (Philippians 4:19). Why not commit your needs to Him who is able now and ask Him daily to give you your daily bread and lead you to the person with the right provision to bless you?

CHAPTER FIVE

The wind Beneath My wings

I'm sure you have heard some matchmaking stories that turned out well and others that didn't turn out so well. Chapter 3 of Ruth is where we get into the romance part of the book. Naomi says to Ruth after sensing Boaz's interest, "*My daughter, shall I not seek security for you, that it may be well with you?*" (verse 1). In other words, Shall I not find a husband for you? "*Now is not Boaz our kinsman, with whose maids you were? Behold, he winnows barley at the threshing floor tonight*" (verse 2). Here's Naomi the matchmaker, "Matchmaker, matchmaker, make me a match." Wait a minute. Don't think Naomi was just some meddling mother-in-law here. Naomi wasn't meddling. She was only looking out for Ruth's best interests.

Advice on getting a Man

So she said, "Sit down, girl. Let me give you four pieces of advice on getting a man."
1. Take a bath. I don't think I need to say more here. She said, "*Behold, he winnows barley at*

the threshing floor tonight. Wash yourself therefore" (verse 3–4). It's kind of like party time after the winnowing.

2. Anoint yourself. She told Ruth to put on some Eternity or Chanel No. 5 or the Moab Midnight perfume she brought with her. So, look good and smell good. By the way, this is very important advice. You will be amazed at how spiritual some ladies can be that they forget how they look. Boaz may be spiritually minded, but he has a nose too. You eligible bachelors, you need to know that a lady who loves the Lord may also want a nice-looking gentleman. It is low class to hide beneath the disguise of spirituality.

3. Put on your best clothing. What she is saying there is "Ruth, I think it's time for you to take off your widow's dress you've been wearing since you lost your husband in Moab, and now is the time to put on the dress for the wedding." It's time for Ruth to exchange her sorrow for the joy of the Lord, because God has something else special for her yet.

Maybe you have been mourning the husband or wife you used to have too. Or maybe you have been grieving the relationship that got away from you. Sometimes in life you have to be willing to let go. You can't hang on to dead things when God says He is *"the God of Abraham, the God of Isaac, and the God of Jacob"* (Exodus 3:15) and not "I was the God of the dead."

4. Get down on it. *"It shall be when he lies down, that you shall notice the place where he lies, and you shall go and uncover his feet and lie down"* (verse 4).

I know what you might be thinking now with a Black Eyed Peas song ringing in your ears. "I gotta feeling that tonight's gonna be a good, good night." No! You got the wrong feeling. This is no soap opera. There is no hanky-panky here. You know why? Because the threshing floor where they were lying down was an open public square. It was really out in the open. That tells me they couldn't have been making out. This was no *Jersey Shore*.

Moreover, the text says what it means. Ruth uncovered the feet of Boaz—not his chest, not his waist, but his feet. The last I checked in Hebrew lexicon, *feet* means "feet." So then, what does it mean for Ruth to uncover Boaz's feet?

Imagine this: Ruth comes in at night, and Boaz is snoring. She crawls under his covers, startles Boaz, who says "Who is this under my covers?" (see verse 9). Sheepishly, Ruth answers, "It's me." And she says to him, because she is in the right place with the right person, "Cover me under your wings!"

To spread your covering over a maiden is a Hebrew idiom. It is a Hebrew way of saying "Marry me." Here Ruth was proposing to Boaz, and nothing more was happening under the covers. No one-night stand. In a beautiful way Ruth was saying something romantic and yet redemptive. She was saying, "Boaz, I want you to be my kinsman redeemer. I want you to be the wind beneath my wings." In other words, "Boaz, you be the answer to your own prayers that you prayed for me while we were back in the field" (see Ruth 2:12).

Like Ruth, if you are willing to follow Naomi's advice by prettying up yourself, taking off your widow's dress and letting go of your past disappointments, the word of the Lord to you from Isaiah 61:3 is the fourth favour factor He is getting ready to bring to you if you will trust Him with your situation.

#4. God's favour will Bring you to the Right partnership

Isaiah 61:3 says the Lord wants to give you *"beauty for ashes, the oil of joy for mourning, the garment of praise for the spirit of heaviness"* (KJV). When God's anointing is on you, you don't have to force a thing. You don't have to manipulate your way into anything. There is an anointing that makes everything flow easily. So, Ruth, put on that one special dress for your Boaz! The wedding bells are about to ring.

By the way, how Naomi was telling Ruth to dress for her Boaz is no way suggesting seduction. There is something called "indecent exposure" in the way many young ladies dress today, and Ruth's advice was far from that.

Parents, it may be a good idea to start praying for God to bring the right spouse to your child. Marian and I pray for our four children that, as God is preparing them now, He will be preparing whoever they are going to marry too. My parents prayed that prayer for me.

I remember when I called my father and mother in Nigeria to tell them that I had found this beautiful, gorgeous girl who was making my heart beat fast and I wanted to ask her to marry me. I'll never forget what my parents asked me. They didn't say, "Oh, is she black or white?" They didn't ask, "Is she Nigerian or Canadian?" All they asked was "Is she a Christian girl?" That's a good question to ask your children too! It's a question steeped in a deep faith in God's grace and not in the human race.

Do you know that the book of Ruth is really a story of what God has done for you too? The Bible says God the Father looked down on you and saw how badly you need to be redeemed. You were once lost and without hope. You had no way of meeting up with Jesus. Just like Ruth you were a stranger (Ephesians 2:12). And God the Father said, "What shall I do?" He turned to Gabriel. He looked also to Michael the archangel for the answer. But the Bible says that heaven was silent for about half an hour (Revelation 8:1). Then the Father's eyes caught the eyes of His Son. Time and destiny kissed each other as the Father said, "I will send My Son for Tai, I will send My Son for _____ (put your name there), to be their Redeemer. But if He is going to be their Redeemer, He must first be their kinsman." Hence the Bible says, "*The Word became flesh, and dwelt among us*" (John 1:14). He was born in Bethlehem's manger—Jesus Christ, our Kinsman Redeemer! Thank God we have a Redeemer.

As we move on to the next chapter, allow me to pause and ask you a destiny-altering question. Is

Jesus your Redeemer today? If He is not, you can meet with Him right where you are. Just say this simple prayer: "Lord Jesus, thank You for coming to earth to pay the penalty for my sin. I ask You to forgive me, and in faith I trust You for my salvation. Amen!" Praise God that you have claimed Jesus as your Kinsman Redeemer too!

prayer guide

You don't want to settle for second best. Settle for God's best. You can do so by including in your prayer for God to raise up the right partner for you in your business or in your selection of a mate.

CHAPTER SIX

Happily Ever After

I was just thinking about a little jingle I heard this week. It goes like this: "Sally and Johnny sitting in a tree, K-I-S-S-I-N-G. First comes love, then comes marriage, then comes Sally pushing a baby carriage." In the first chapter of Ruth we have destiny decisions, and in the second chapter we have love, and in the third we have marriage. Now, as we come to the fourth chapter of Ruth, we have a baby carriage. What a story! What an answer to prayer!

I'd like to say that after Ruth proposed to Boaz (like my wife proposed to me), that was the end of the story, and they got married and they lived happily ever after. But I can't tell you that, because the story is not quite finished yet. The Boaz prayer is about to take an even more interesting turn. There is a little problem in this romance.

Sometimes when it seems your prayers are being answered, other challenges crop up. Before Boaz could say to Ruth, "I take thee, Ruth, to be my lawful wedded wife...to cherish...for better or for

worse, for richer or for poorer"—you know, men, all
the vows we have to say to our brides-to-be—before
Boaz could ask Ruth to be his wife, here is the jinx,
here is the twist and turn of this Cinderella story:
there is another man in the picture.

I know you like stories with happy endings.
Everybody loves happy-ending stories since the
days when we enjoyed having nursery storybooks
read to us. "And Prince Charming and Cinderella
rode off on a horse into the beautiful sunset…and
they lived happily ever after." But don't get carried
away yet, because the whole story has to be told.

See, what makes a happy ending is a messy middle. We all want to jump to the happy ending part,
but if you've lived long enough you'll know that
what makes a happy ending a happy ending is the
messy middle. We won't say it was a happy ending
if there wasn't a messy middle. The messy middle is
what makes it a happy ending!

People are jealous of you now because they can
see the glory of God in your life. They see the glory,
but they don't know the story. The glory comes
with the story. Go
ahead; if you want **The glory comes with the story.**
my glory, go ahead
and have it—knock yourself out, but I need to tell
you, you can't have the glory without the story,
because like love and marriage, they "go together
like a horse and carriage." And "you can't have one
without the other."

So, simply put, behind every glory there is a
story, there is a struggle, there is a test, and God

designs it that way so that after all you've been through, you now can say, "You know what? It was good for me that I have been afflicted; for had I not been afflicted the way I was afflicted, I wouldn't have known the Lord like I know Him now." I am glad that everyone counted me out. I'm glad life wasn't a bed of roses. I had to struggle and press through the crowd like the woman with the issue of blood. But, oh! I'm sure happy that God still writes the last chapter of the book of my life.

So here was Ruth. She thought Boaz was her man, and now she had to hear Boaz say, "There's another man!" "*I am a close relative; however...*" (Ruth 3:12). Has somebody ever looked you in the eye and said, "I love you, but ..."? Boaz said to Ruth, "I'm a close redeemer, but I'm not the closest. There's another man in the picture."

If you've ever been dumped, I think you know how Ruth must have felt here. Her achy breaky heart must have sunk again. I can imagine Ruth thinking, "And what does this other relative look like? I hope he is not a little weasel. Why can't it be you?"

But, praise God, Boaz wasn't about to just give up and walk away like that. Because true love doesn't give up! The Bible says in 1 Corinthians 13:13, "*And now abide faith, hope, love, these three; but the greatest of these is love*" (NKJV). Everything else can fail, but love never fails! Although the law of the kinsman redeemer said the closest relative was the one who could redeem Ruth, Boaz was not about to give her up, so he took this other man to court.

In the opening of chapter 4, the text says, "*Now Boaz went up to the gate and sat down there, and behold, the close relative of whom Boaz spoke was passing by*" (verse 1). The gate was the courthouse back then, where matters were settled. Now people go to Judge Judy, but back then you went before the elders at the city gate.

So Boaz began to present his case. He said, "There's a piece of land that Naomi and her husband sold before they went to Moab. Now, as the kinsman redeemer, the law says you are the one to buy it back" (see verses 3-4). So when this guy heard real estate, he was thinking "Money! Money! Money!" At the end of verse 4 he said, "*I will redeem it.*"

By this time Boaz was praying, "Oh no! Lord, please don't let him." But he wasn't about to give up yet! Then Boaz said, "By the way, whoever gets the land also gets the wife" (see verse 5). And the guy exclaimed, "No! I can't do that!" They didn't have prenuptial agreements back then. Oh, this other guy loved the idea of owning real estate, but the idea of a wife coming with the package—that was another matter.

It reminds me of an ad in a local newspaper. The ad reads, "Farmer looking for a wife. She must own a tractor. She doesn't have to be good-looking, but she must own a tractor. If interested please send picture of tractor to P.O. Box 211..."

Isn't if funny how people want what you have, but they are too dumb to see that love and marriage goes together like a horse and carriage...and you can't have one without the other! Yes! You can't have one without the other. You can't have the land without Ruth!

Thank God we have a willing redeemer, who is God's own Son! Precious Lamb of God, Messiah. His name is Jesus! The Bible says, when He saw us on the slave market, offered up to be sold, while we were still helpless, nowhere to turn to, nobody wanted us, but at the right time Jesus Christ, our kinsman redeemer, came along and said, "I want him, and him and her and her and him…"

Just when we were about to say, "Oh no! Stop the story! This isn't going to be a happy ending!" the other guy in the picture said to Boaz in verse 6, *"Redeem it for yourself; you may have my right of redemption, for I cannot redeem it."*

Can you picture Boaz doing the holy cartwheels in his heart, going, "Yes! A wed-ding! Finally I can put a ring on Ruth's finger." But the story isn't finished yet, because God is still writing the final chapter. Just because your life is a messy middle right now doesn't mean you can't finish with a happy ending.

The devil is a liar. No matter where you are in your journey coming out of Moab, if you love God and trust in His word, the best is yet to come for you.

Two Great Expectations

Here are two things you can expect in your final chapter, like Ruth.

1. Time for Birthing in the Right place

I heard Bishop T. D. Jakes speak once about the necessity of birthing in a healthy place. Animals don't give birth in traffic; they don't give birth where there's chaos. They don't give birth when they are being attacked left and right. No! They give birth in a place of safety, in a healthy place, in the right place. Many of you ladies who have gone through childbirth can also testify to the importance of birthing in a healthy place.

What God is about to teach us in this last chapter of Ruth is incredible. Watch this: "*So Boaz took Ruth, and she became his wife, and he went in to her. And the Lord enabled her to conceive, and she gave birth to a son*" (Ruth 4:13). She what? She gave birth to a son! Now we have the baby carriage part of our story. Now we are talking baby talk!

Why is this an incredible ending? I'll tell you why. Here's Ruth on her second marriage, to Boaz, finally having her first pregnancy because she's finally healthy enough to reproduce. We know in chapter 1 when she was in Moab for 10 years with her first husband that she was not able to conceive. But now that she's in the right place with the right person, God says to her, "Now I am going to let you do what you couldn't do before."

Could it be that God is saying to you too that now that you have cleaned up your act, now that you have kissed your Moab goodbye and now that you know who God is and you know who you are and whose you are, you can now get ready to give birth to your dream in a healthy place? He did it once for Ruth, and He can do it again! I am not just talking about giving birth to physical babies. I am talking about giving birth to new businesses, new ministries, going back to school for your master's degree.

Isaiah 54:1 says, "'*Shout for joy, O barren one, you who have borne no child; Break forth into joyful shouting and cry aloud, you who have not travailed; For the sons of the desolate one will be more numerous Than the sons of the married woman,' says the Lord.*" Today, I declare it over you, get ready to birth whatever you have been pregnant with, because now you are in a healthy atmosphere. Now you have the peace of God reigning in your life.

Seven years ago when we came to our present church, we had a sign up that said, "It's Time To Build." We thought that was the time to build, as the congregation was poised for a fresh start. But the events of the last few years had proven that we were not really ready to build yet. The church needed to be in a healthy place first before our Boaz prayer

IF YOU HAVE THE COURAGE LIKE RUTH TO REDO WHAT YOU FAILED AT BEFORE, GOD'S PROMISE IS THAT HE WILL OPEN UP YOUR "WOMB" AND BLESS YOU TO BE PRODUCTIVE IN AREAS WHERE YOU WERE ONCE UNPRODUCTIVE.

could be answered. Now that our minds are no longer distracted, now that we have our focus back, now that we have a vision and renewed strength, we are in a rebuilding program now at my church.

Here is the crux of what I am saying to you: If you have the courage like Ruth to redo what you failed at before, God's promise is that He will open up your "womb" and bless you to be productive in areas where you were once unproductive. It won't matter that it took 10 years to birth that baby. So it took you a little longer to get that degree. The race is never for the swift. You might be 40 years old or as old as Methuselah. Let me tell you what the Bible says: *"The latter glory of this house will be greater than the former"* (Haggai 2:9).

Here is the second great expectation in your final chapter.

2. Time for God to Work all Things out

"Then the women said to Naomi, 'Blessed is the LORD who has not left you without a redeemer today'" (Ruth 4:14). God has not left Naomi without a what? A redeemer! *"Then Naomi took the child and laid him in her lap"* (Ruth 4:16). Hah! Can you see how the Lord is working it all out in Naomi's life? It's not just Ruth who is getting blessed. Naomi too is reaping the Boaz prayer. This was the same woman who said, *"Do not call me Naomi [pleasant]; call me Mara [bitter], for the Almighty has dealt very bitterly with me. I went out full, but the LORD has brought me back empty"* (Ruth 1:20). Often, like Naomi, we

are tempted to look at one piece of the puzzle rather than gain a whole perspective of what God is up to in our lives. Like Peter, just because we didn't catch fish all night doesn't mean we can't have a catch if we try again (Luke 5:4–8).

Who told you, Naomi, to change your name? When the Lord called you "Pleasant" it was because He declared that your life would end in joy. Though it may have a messy middle, it will have a happy ending! Naomi, just because it didn't happen for you in Moab doesn't mean God is not able.

If your story is like Ruth and Naomi's story, the good news for you is that God isn't finished with you yet either. The Lord Almighty is still writing the final chapter of your story, so don't go around throwing yourself a pity party like Naomi did.

Think with me for a moment. The real message of this book is that Naomi was wrong anyway. She didn't come back empty. Ruth didn't die in Moab! Ruth came back with Naomi. Even now in retrospect the village women could say Ruth was better to Naomi than seven sons (Ruth 4:15).

Guess who else didn't die in Moab? God! God wasn't dead in Moab. You may not see it, but when you think God isn't at work in your life, that's when He is doing His most awesome work. Naomi just thought she had lost everything in Moab. And if you let the enemy trick you too, he'll make you become bitter and tell you that all hope is lost. However, I implore you, don't believe the devil's lies. If you can just let go of your bitterness and let God, the Word of the

Lord says in Joel 2:25, "*I will restore to you the years that the locust hath eaten, the cankerworm, and the caterpiller, and the palmerworm*" (KJV).

I don't want your story to be like Jack's story. Jack was being chased by a tiger. Jack ran as fast as he could until he came to the edge of a cliff with the tiger still chasing him. With nowhere to go, Jack looked over the edge of the cliff and saw a branch growing out of the side of the cliff a few feet below. So he jumped down and grabbed the branch just as the tiger reached where he was. The tiger growled as Jack sighed a great sigh of relief.

Just then a mouse came out from a hole and began to chew on the branch. My man Jack looked down, and he saw what was a drop of a thousand feet and sure death. So he looked up to the heavens and yelled, "Dear God, if You are there, please help! I'll do anything You ask, but please help."

Suddenly, a voice came booming down. "You'll do anything I ask?"

Jack, shocked to hear a reply, yelled back, "I'll do anything, but please save me!" By this time, the branch had begun to weaken from the mouse chewing on it, and the tiger was still growling on top. So Jack pleaded more. "Please, Lord, tell me what I must do and I will do it. Your will is my will."

Then the voice from heaven said, "Okay, in that case, let go of the branch."

My man looked down to a fall of a thousand feet, looked up at the hungry tiger, looked down, looked up again. There was a long silence. Then he yelled, "Is there anyone else up there?"

Have you ever felt like Jack? We say we want to "Let go and let God," but as soon as we find out that what He is asking us to go through is too difficult to handle, we go back to Moab.

No! To be a believer means that you trust and obey, for there's no other way to be happy in Jesus than to trust and obey!

Trusting God is a wonderful thing. It's so wonderful to just say, "I don't understand how it would all work out!" Ruth had to let go of her dreams for God's dreams. But if you had told Ruth in Moab that her latter days were going to be better than her former, she would have said, "What are you talking about, Wallace?" She wouldn't have been able to see through her shattered dreams, but Romans 8:28 says, *"And we know that God causes all things to work together for good to those who love God, to those who are called according to His purpose."*

No, it doesn't say that all things feel good, all things seem good. It doesn't say that all things look good. But it says God has a way of using all things, even the things the enemy brings against you. God says, "I'm going to take all things and make them work for your good." Even the abuse, even the misuse, even the misfortune, everything they meant for evil to destroy you, God says, if you'll just hold on tight till the end and trust Him, He'll carry you through as He did Ruth and Naomi. Oh, I'm a witness! Our God is a God of restoration! As the old hymn says, "Through it all I have learned to trust in Jesus..."

If this story of Ruth had just ended in a little Judean village with an old grandma, Naomi, holding a new grandson on her lap, I would still have called it a happy ending. I would still have said, "And they lived happily ever after." But praise God, the person who wrote the book of Ruth didn't know half of what was still going to happen, because this story is about to come to an incredible climax. Verse 17 says, "*The neighbor women gave him a name, saying, 'A son has been born to Naomi!' So they named him Obed.*" *Obed* means "worshipper."

Oh! I'm not finished yet! Keep reading: "*So they named him Obed. He is the father of Jesse, the father of David.*" The father of who? The father of David. That's right!

And then in verse 18 on, the author begins to list the names of all these genealogies of who begat who. The reason why I said the person who wrote this book didn't know how happily ever after this story would actually end is because 30 generations later, 28 "greats" (go ahead, start counting, *great, great, great, great, great...great* grandson) and 30 great-grands later, Jesus the Messiah, our Lord, was born into this incredible family of Ruth and Boaz! That's how happily ever after this story was.

All these then resulted in in God's great providential plan so that Matthew the Gospel writer wrote, "*Salmon was the father of Boaz by Rahab*" (Matthew 1:5). By who? So Rahab, the harlot, was Boaz's mother! "*Boaz was the father of Obed by Ruth, and Obed the father of Jesse. Jesse was the father of David the king*" (verses 5-6)!

Why did I bring you here to the New Testament to end this chapter? I brought you here because you need to know one more time that if you are a believer, your past will never determine your destiny. What will determine your future is your God! If Rahab can be in this story, then there is hope for you!

prayer guide

As you make plans for the future, pray that everything you do will result in God's providential plan coming to fruition in your life.

CHAPTER SEVEN

waiting in line at christmas

Do you have a wait problem? I don't mean w-e-i-g-h-t problem. I mean, how patient are you in waiting for anything? If you put yourself on a waiting scale from 1 to 10, with 1 being so impatient that you don't know what the word *patience* means, to 10, meaning you're a carefree person and you don't own a watch, where would you be on the scale?

I used to think I was a patient man until I got married and then started having children. Four children! And the reason we have four is because my wife doesn't want five. I am working on my impatience. If you'd like to join me, I am starting a group called "Impatient Anonymous." The meeting starts right now!

Jokes aside, the first item on the agenda is that we all have to confess that we have some wait problems. If there was ever any impatient generation that ever lived, it is this generation of ours. More and more we are trying to figure out ways to beat our rat race in this instant gratification society. And instead of life flowing better, have you noticed it's getting crazier? Do you remember the time when McDonald's had only one window? Now you've got to drive to the first stop and order, then you drive up to the first window to pay, then they tell you to drive up to another window to pick up your McChicken.

My impatience gets tested in a lot of places, especially around Christmas. I get frustrated waiting in line at the local Wal-Mart. That's why three years ago Marian and I decided to not to go do our Christmas shopping in the middle of the day. Never again. Now we wake up at 3 o'clock in the middle of the night to go shop hassle free. I may live longer than some of you that way!

No doubt we live in an instamatic generation. We are in a hurry for everything, including getting our prayers answered. But have you noticed that God isn't in a hurry? At times I even feel that God has gone out of His way to arrange things so I have to wait a lot. I am just being honest, if that's okay. I know it's hard to see the good that can come from waiting. But oh! What an awesome privilege to be counted worthy of waiting on the Lord.

In this world of instant gratification, if there is one thing that's worth our wait, it's God! He may not show up when you want

> As believers the one thing we know for certain is, God is never in a hurry, but He is never late either. He is the on-time God!

Him to show up. He may not come to you like you want Him to come, walking on water. In the meantime, you may have to wait for this thing or that thing you have been praying for. As believers the one thing we know for certain is, God is never in a hurry, but He is never late either. He is the on-time God!

What I am pointing out to you is that the very essence of prayer itself involves waiting. A request is made, and an answer is giving to the request, whether yes, no or wait. You have to be a good waiter to be a prayer warrior. Rarely do you find a prayer answered quickly in the Bible. I counted 12 times where the word *wait* is connected to prayer in the Bible, especially in the psalms. There is usually a waiting time, when our resolve is being tested.

I am glad that God hasn't always given me what I have asked for when I asked for it. There have been times when if God had granted my request right away, I would have messed my life up. Why? Because I wasn't ready for the thing I was asking for even though I thought I was.

When my son Adam was 16 years old, he wanted me to buy him a car. He sure felt he was ready to start driving. But being a responsible father I knew if I granted his request he would hurt himself. Moreover, I knew he wasn't ready to handle the responsibilities of owning a car (like paying for the insurance, buying gas and doing repairs).

Similarly, our heavenly Father knows what is best for His children, and He grants our requests when He sees fit. Oh, if only we could see the good side of waiting! I confess I am getting better at waiting. But how do you learn to wait?

The Bible is filled with waiters. As we draw the message of this book to a final conclusion, we cannot write a book about prayer without also gaining deeper understanding of the power of waiting on unanswered prayer. So while you are waiting for God's providential plan to unfold in your life, to give you help and encouragement in your time of waiting I want to leave you with four people in the Bible who waited in line at Christmas.

Boaz, waiting to Determine God's will

The first person in waiting in line is Boaz. It's incredible the amount of waiting that runs through the book of Ruth. The book starts with an impatient family who couldn't wait on God. They were so impatient, like Abraham, that they left a place of God's blessing in Bethlehem and took off to Moab, a cursed place. Then as we come to chapter 3 of Ruth, just as things started looking up for Ruth, Ruth and Boaz finally met, and it looked as if this was going to be a marriage made in heaven, the shoe dropped. Has the shoe ever dropped on you? You have been waiting for that husband or wife, you've been waiting in line for that promotion at work or that business deal, and the next thing you know—you get dumped.

It didn't seem like Ruth and Boaz were going to jump on the horse and ride into the sunset, because there was another man in the picture (Ruth 3:12). Here was Boaz, who by now was probably over 60 years old, never married, had his hopes up but now has to wait to see if he would ever get married or be a confirmed bachelor for life. But there was somebody else waiting in line in this book.

Naomi, waiting to Discover God's will

This is even more interesting than the first. Here's Naomi the matchmaker, Naomi the e-harmony.com, Naomi the Christian Mingle.com, who had sent Ruth off to the floor to go "git down on it" with Boaz (you remember, nothing immoral, nothing sexual). But here is Naomi. She sent Ruth off on a date, and she is sitting at home and has no idea of what is going on at the threshing floor. They didn't have cellphones back then. She didn't get a text message from the threshing floor as to how it was all going down. Ruth couldn't BBM Naomi. No, Naomi had to wait to discover God's will in this matter until Ruth got home and even after.

Parents, you know what that is like, those of you who have kids old enough to date. Sometimes they go out on a date with a guy or girl you are crazy about. Other times, you know they are going out with somebody you are not so crazy about. And you are watching and waiting and secretly praying that the guy will find another girl and dump your daughter. Don't pretend that you don't know what I'm talking about.

So when Ruth finally got back home, Naomi said to her, "How did it go, girl?" Or, as the King James version puts it, "*Who art thou, my daughter?*" (Ruth 3:16). By that Naomi wasn't saying, "Who are you?" as though she didn't know who Ruth was. Rather, it was a Hebrew idiom, meaning "Are you now Mrs. Boaz?" Nevertheless, Naomi had to wait as this dramatic episode unfolded.

And then somebody else had to wait too.

Ruth, waiting to do God's will

The third person to wait in line was Ruth. After Ruth told Naomi all that went on, that Boaz couldn't pop the question to her yet, Naomi said to Ruth, "*Wait, my daughter*" (Ruth 3:18). That's our word, *wait*. Oh! It is tough to do! It's hard to sit still waiting when your biological clock is ticking. It's tough to wait when you want what you want and you want it now! It's like the lady who was praying to God to give her patience and said, "Lord, please give me patience, and I want it now!"

Chances are you too are in a situation right now where you are waiting for a prayer to be answered. Maybe since you picked up this book you have been on a Boaz prayer, and nothing is happening that you can see. You are single, and Mr. Right or Miss Right is still not knocking on your door.

WAIT ON THE LORD!

86

If you have done all you can, I'll tell you one more thing you can do: Wait on the Lord! While you are waiting, work on being the right person, like Ruth, because when you do, God will surely bring you to that right person, to your Boaz, if that's His will for you. I did some waiting to in my single years. I often say to people in my premarital counselling that God didn't bring Eve to Adam until He knew Adam was ready. And God won't bring your Boaz to you until He knows you have done all to stand (Ephesians 6:13).

But here is where I'm going with these three people so far. You are probably wondering by now, what does Boaz's, Naomi's and Ruth's waiting have to do with Christmas? I'll tell you.

Imagine how things could have turned out if Boaz, Naomi and Ruth were not willing to wait on the Lord but took matters into their own hands. If they had not waited, there could have been a break in the genealogy of Christ. Just think of that. However, because they were good waiters, praise God, nearly a century later when Matthew the writer of the first Gospel sat down to write the list of the who's who of the Christmas story (those who waited in line for Christmas), guess who were there? Boaz and Ruth (Matthew 1:5)! So there is great blessing that comes to those who wait.

Ruth and Boaz not only got married, but the Lord also blessed their union with the gift of a son, as we saw in the previous chapter. And Obed would later become the grandfather of King David, the ancestor of our Lord Jesus Christ. No wonder

David himself bore witness to the truth that there is a way to see the goodness of the Lord in the land of the living, and that way, he said, is to wait upon the Lord (Psalm 27:13). Don't wait for Santa at Christmas! Don't wait for the government to come bail you out either! But instead wait on the Lord, be strong and let your heart take courage. Yes, wait for the Lord!

simeon, waiting to disclose god's will

Here comes my last waiter in line at Christmas, Simeon. Fast forward now; it's thousands of years later from the time of Boaz, Ruth and Naomi, our other three waiters. You won't find this part of the Christmas story in many pageants. In comes Simeon (Luke 2). Dr. Luke says, "*And, behold, there was a man in Jerusalem, whose name was Simeon…waiting*" (Luke 2:25, KJV). That's our word again, *waiting*. We are not sure when Simeon was told that "*he should not see death, before he had seen the Lord's Christ*" (verse 26). Perhaps it was revealed to him when he was 20 or 30 or 50 years old. But now he is in his late 80s. Think of how long he has been waiting, waiting and expecting Jesus to come. Are you still expecting? Whatever you may be expecting, expectation can be nerve-racking.

Imagine you are Simeon walking on the street on a normal afternoon, and you know you won't die until you see the Christ child. Then suddenly, the Holy Spirit says to you, "Go to the temple; it's

time! It's time for you to see the Lord's Christ."
How would you feel? You probably have a much
different bucket list of things you would like to do
before you die, like see the Grand Canyon or go
skydiving. Simeon wasn't looking to do any of
that! The Bible tells us that he had lived his whole
life looking for one thing and one thing only, to
see Jesus!

Can you see the old man moving slowly up the
temple stairs, at just the right time, on just the right
day when Mary and Joseph were bringing baby
Jesus to the temple? Now picture this: there were
many couples at the temple that day who came to
dedicate their children (Luke 2). Have you ever
wondered how Simeon was able to pick Jesus out of
the crowd of crying babies? The answer: the Holy
Spirit! It was the Holy Spirit that revealed to
Simeon, "This is the One! The Desire of nations.
The long-expected Jesus, born to set His people
free!" What the Word of God is teaching us here is,
while we are waiting on the Lord, God

...WHILE WE ARE WAITING ON THE
LORD, GOD WILL REVEAL THINGS TO
US TOO.

will reveal things to us too. The closer you walk
with the Lord, the more He'll disclose things to
you (see Proverbs 3:5–6).

The Bible says Simeon held baby Jesus up for
all to see, and he said, "*Lord, now lettest thou thy ser-
vant depart in peace, according to thy word: For mine eyes
have seen thy salvation*" (Luke 2:29–30, KJV). What a
way to end a life, by disclosing the will of God for

all to see! Simeon disclosed God's will for all to see. And that's what God intends the Boaz prayer to be in your life too.

If you take anything with you from these four waiters as you wait in line for your Boaz prayers to be answered, let it be this: With God all things are possible for those who believe (see Mark 10:27). He may not come to you in the

WITH GOD ALL THINGS ARE POSSIBLE FOR THOSE WHO BELIEVE.

morning. He may not come to you in the noonday break or in your midnight hour. But as surely as the sun will rise, He will come to you. I declare it over you, you will fulfill your destiny in Jesus' name. This is the season of miracles. Yours is coming too!

"Wait for the LORD; Be strong and let your heart take courage; Yes, wait for the LORD" (Psalm 27:14). He will come! Because He is worthy, why don't you go ahead and give Him your best praise, now that your Boaz prayer is being answered?

CASTLE QUAY BOOKS

OTHER AWARD WINNING CASTLE QUAY
TITLES INCLUDE:

Bent Hope (Tim Huff)

The Beautiful Disappointment (Colin McCartney)

The Cardboard Shack Beneath the Bridge (Tim Huff)

Certainty (Grant Richison) - **NEW!**

Dancing with Dynamite
(Tim Huff) - **NEW! 2011 Book of the Year Award!**

Deciding to Know God in a Deeper Way
(Sam Tita) - **NEW!**

The Defilers (Deborah Gyapong)

Father to the Fatherless (Paul Boge)

Find a Broken Wall (Brian Stiller) - **NEW!**

Hope for the Hopeless (Paul Boge) - **NEW!**

I Sat Where They Sat (Arnold Bowler)

Jesus and Caesar (Brian Stiller)

Keep On Standing (Darlene Polachic)

The Leadership Edge (Elaine Stewart-Rhude)

Leaving a Legacy (David C. Bentall) - **NEW!**

Making Your Dreams Your Destiny (Judy Rushfeldt)

Mentoring Wisdom (Dr. Carson Pue) - **NEW!**

Mere Christian (Michael Coren)

One Smooth Stone (Marcia Lee Laycock)

Predators Live Among Us: Protect Your Family from
Child Sex Abuse (Diane Roblin-Lee) - **NEW!**

Red Letter Revolution (Colin McCartney)

Reflections (Cal Bombay) - **NEW!**

www.ingramcontent.com/pod-product-compliance
Lightning Source LLC
Chambersburg PA
CBHW052159090426

42741CB00010B/2332